7 HABITS
TO BUILDING
A SUCCESSFUL
BUSINESS

WHAT CAN I CREATE? WHO CAN I SERVE?

Two questions that change everything

INDY AGNIHOTRI

Copyright © 2018 Indy Agnihotri

All rights reserved. No part of this publication may be reproduced or transmitted in any form or by any means, electronic, mechanical, photocopying, recording or otherwise without prior permission of the author.

Design by: Noir

This book is for those who are:

– Setting up in business for the first time

– Struggling to know how to grow their business

– Wondering what the most important things are to create a successful business

I should know I was asking the same questions a few years ago…

About the author

I provide accounting, finance director and business coaching services to small medium enterprises, utilising my skills as an experienced Chartered Accountant and my extensive previous corporate experience working for London consultancy firms.

In recent years, I have followed my passion of providing advice to owner-managed businesses and entrepreneurs. I love supporting them build their businesses into successful and often multi-million pound business operations.

I also lecture on a part-time basis in business which I find personally rewarding, and have a strong interest in working with social enterprises having worked overseas for Mohammed Yunus (founder of Microfinance and Nobel Peace Prize Winner).

I have a real passion for service and providing assistance – whether that is for businesses, students, individuals and basically anyone with the ambition to fulfil their potential. It is that hidden potential in people that I love assisting in bringing out.

Wherever you are at your stage in your business, if you have the drive to want to succeed and have a strong bias for action, contact me and we can have a conversation.

"Remember – we live one life, one time to use the skills and potential we have to do what we really want."

Indy Agnihotri

Business Coach/Consultant,
Strategic Finance Director, Trainer

indy@business-advance.co.uk
www.business-advance.co.uk | www.leadabetterlife.co.uk

Preface to 2017 reprinted edition

It has been some 3 years since I initially wrote this book and a lot has happened since then, both personally and business-wise.

This includes not only experiencing many successes in businesses I have worked with, but also their failures (and this equally applies to my own business). As you will read later, this combination is the path to overall success.

All this has also meant the messages in this book are even more meaningful and powerful to me than they were before.

I have now titled this Volume 1 for a reason, Volume 2 is in the process of being written and will look at more practical ways of building a business – something clients and business-owners ask me often, and I feel now is the right time to share this with you.

You will note that I have changed the sub-title of this book to *"What can I create? Who can I serve? Two questions that change everything."*

I feel this really sums up the book's message. Creation and service are the two elements that underpin a successful business. And also a successful life.

Enjoy the read.

Do these 7 things and it will change
EVERYTHING

11
A new way of thinking

13
1. Serve not sell
It's all about them

19
2. It's all about value, value, value
Not price

25
3. Create vs being reported on
Will you take control of your destiny AND take action to create it?

29
4. Feel the fear... and do it anyway
Are you willing to collect more 'No's' then anyone else?

33
5. Leadership
In yourself and others

37
6. The power of language
Questions, questions, questions

43
7. Support
Do what you do best and outsource the rest

47
What do you do and where do you go next?
What is the first thing you should do right NOW

51
The 7 step action plan to get you started
The key is start

A NEW WAY OF THINKING

"The only way to do great work is to LOVE what you do"

– Steve Jobs

A NEW WAY OF THINKING

This book brings a new way of thinking to growing your business and creating new clients. I use the word 'creating' for a reason (I'll explain that later).

'In simple terms, serve your clients so powerfully and authentically that they are impacted by what you and your business is offering. And remember it's never just about the business.'

This is not a classic sales book, nor is it a 'how-to' book. It is really a book on my experience of what it takes to really impact clients so powerfully that they want to do business with you.

I should know, I was struggling to make a living for 2 years. Then I started learning and reached out to get support. I wanted to know how to master creating and growing a business successfully. So I read and read, hired an amazing coach (really he was amazing), and practiced, practiced, practiced.

At the end of it all (and by no means is it really the end), I came to the conclusions in this book. And my learning continues to grow.

It is important to state that in my journey I also failed enough times. Failure to me is just as important as success, as through the path of failure and feedback you learn and develop. And then you eventually succeed. Failure for me still happens of course but just at another level as I continue to push my boundaries. However, I also hope by learning and implementing the key principles in this book, you will avoid some of the hard lessons I learnt and fail much less than I did.

My mentors have been John P Morgan and Rich Litvin who have been instrumental in bringing the ideas in this book to life (my life). While the key principles are great (and life changing) the main focus and message to you is ACTION, go out and implement what you learn.

Even if you do a few of the 7 areas I mention here in this book, it will change EVERYTHING.

HABIT ONE

SERVE NOT SELL

It's all about them

Door to door

Don't you hate the door to door salesman approach to selling? I really do. It is aggressive, false and in-human like (or maybe you do like it, if so you're reading the wrong book).

Just yesterday, someone tried to sell to me. Within 5 minutes, he was asking me to sign a contract, saying the review he had carried out of my financial affairs *'had passed the test'*. I said I needed to think about it.

Another time, while acting on behalf of a client, a firm was being aggressive, phoning us every day, asking us to sign a contract by Friday as the deal and special offer would close then (really I wonder why?). The contract value was for £20,000 (reduced by £5,000 if we signed early). We didn't sign and decided to look elsewhere.

As I mention later, *'needy is creepy'*.

For small purchases selling like the above might be more acceptable (although even then I still don't like it). But when someone is paying a relatively large amount for your product or services, you need to do things differently and in my opinion aggressive, door to door sales tactics simply don't work, well not to create a successful business anyway.

So what do you do instead?

Just connect

Just connect with the person you're with when you meet them. Listen to them, ask them questions and look to build a relationship first. Simple. It is just like meeting someone you like and wanting to ask them out on a date. You have to connect first and just get interested in them.

Two ears, one mouth

There is a great story I tell people about what we often don't do in life. If we only did this one thing, it would change everyone's world for the better I assure you.

A dinner guest was speaking to the prime ministers, Disraeli and Gladstone. After speaking to Disraeli, the guest said, *'Wow, Disraeli is the most interesting person I have ever met, he was so interesting, full of story'*. Then later after speaking to Gladstone, the same guest said, *'Wow, after speaking to Gladstone, I felt I was the most interesting person'*.

Be Gladstone. Be *'interested'*, not *'interesting'*.

Get curious about the person in front of you. It is about them not you. It really will change your world if you start to think this way.

Serve not sell

Then what? After you've connected and listened to them, what do you then do? Next, don't sell but 'serve'. Serve the person in front of you.

What do I mean by serving? Well think about the person in front of you in the present moment, and ask yourself 'what would be most beneficial for them and their business?'. If you have been listening, getting curious and asking them the right questions, you will know.

And then, provide an 'experience' of what you can offer the person, impact them powerfully. So if you are offering a service, give them an experience of what that service is, provide some advice upfront. Do what no other competitor of yours would ever do. Stand out and show you really care. And mean it, don't let it be an act. For me the question I often ask at any time is *how can I serve them* in this moment.

What that means, is that sometimes after an initial conversation, I will realise there is not much I can offer them and I leave it at that. And I may never see them again.

Alternatively, if I feel I know I might be able to help them, my conversation will go deeper, deeper than any other person might ever go. At the end of it (but only if it feels right) I may then make a proposal of what it would look like if we worked together.

Sometimes, we may also just keep the conversation alive for weeks, even months. I may think about them and then later send them something of relevance to them. It could be a news article, an email with useful information, or even a book that might be really useful for them. And then, later I may make a proposal to them to work together.

Or I may not.

This is very important. Offer value and service to people – regardless of whether they become an eventual client.

I also mean *'serving'* them and not *'pleasing'* them. Sometimes you have to tell clients the 'truth' even when it makes you and them uncomfortable. You will say things they might not want to hear but it is right for them (ask permission beforehand before you do). Even things that no one has ever said to them before in their lives. And it will change their world for the better.

See the similarity to dating? If not read the above again. It is more similar than you think!

Give and take

And give without the expectation of receiving. A great book, 'Give and Take', talks about there being 3 types of people in the world: 'givers', 'takers' and 'matchers'.

Be a giver (or if you find that hard be at least a matcher). At the same time, be careful who you give to, give to fellow givers and matchers - not to a taker. But start off by giving to everyone but do look out for the takers in life. I've seen a few in my lifetime! And note 'cold' people and 'friendly' people are not necessarily indicators of who a giver or taker is (I learnt this from personal experience the hard way). You need to get to know someone to really see their intentions and actions.

Like most principles, it is just a 'model' of how people are and it is never black or white. But it can be useful when deciding who you want to spend time with.

Needy is creepy

And whatever you do, don't appear too needy for a client. If you don't hear back, leave them be. Send them a gift or note, something that genuinely serves them but don't keep 'chasing' after them (well maybe a little is okay as perseverance is also a good thing!).

> ### Story 1: Serving in action
>
> My client was seeking a sales and marketing firm so we contacted a number of firms:
>
> **Firm 1:** From a 15 minute conversation, Firm 1 sent us an email quote ranging from £15,000 - £25,000. With very little supporting information. They did not ask us many questions nor spend much time with us finding out our needs.
>
> **Firm 2:** Another firm spent a week preparing a document for us which showed that they had researched our company. They also ordered one of our products online to test the online ordering process. Surprisingly, they actually challenged us to think about what we really required (*'serving not pleasing'*). Did we really need a new website for £20,000+ immediately? Maybe we should initially build up sales from the existing website. They suggested a low cost interim solution of £1,000 a month with a 30 day notice period. We immediately felt they cared about us, our business and what we wanted to achieve. We immediately said yes.

> *"The question I ask myself often is how can I serve them in this moment."*

HABIT TWO

IT'S ALL ABOUT VALUE, VALUE, VALUE

Not price

"If there is one thing people want, it's for you to solve their immediate problems. AND more important than that help them reach their secret dream, what they really really want. Help them with that and they will pay whatever you ask"

If there was one thing that changed it all for me, it was this…

Focus on value not price

It took me about a year to really understand and apply it but it has had such an impact on my business. When I got it (AND was able to communicate it) I managed to increase my client fees 10 fold (once recently from £200 to £2,000 a month). Just by focusing on value.

BUT… WARNING!

People will pay, only IF you are actually providing the VALUE. For my client above, I was providing much more than £2,000 of value (I just had not realised it before this and nor had they). But when I did, I got it and so did they.

I told them (authentically) that I had already just saved them £1,500 through cost savings through a few phone calls, and had advised them on tax savings of £4,000 in the last 2 months. This was in my capacity as their accountant. I proposed if this is what I could do on an 'ad hoc' basis, what could I do if I were more formally engaged as their business coach?

I told them in simple terms the concept of 'return on investment'. What this meant was in 'return' for them paying me a fee of £2,000 a month I would assist them in generating 'a return or profit' in excess of the £2,000 fee.

I then actually listed down all the value I could provide them by asking the question to myself and to them, *'what else… what else… can I provide you with more value?'* ('what else' is a favourite question of mine to people, as there is always more under the initial answer – try it).

What was on this list? Well I can do better than that, here are a few of the things I did for them in the initial months.

IT'S ALL ABOUT VALUE, VALUE, VALUE

First some of the 'tangible' value I provided (the things you can measure and quantify):

- Saving them £2,000 on machine purchase negotiated reductions, including accessing new financing options.

- Advised them to increase many of their product prices which generated an additional £1,000 of profit a month, every month.

- Negotiated supplier discounts of 5%-10% on their products and secured £20,000 credit with their suppliers.

Then there was also the intangible benefits. This came through my regular coaching sessions with the directors:

- Empowering them and giving them skills to become leaders in their business.

- Getting them to see their own blind spots and weaknesses which assisted them in operating their business more effectively.

- Through my connections, introducing them to new firms and suppliers and thus giving them access to best practice advice and expertise.

- Assisting them in more effective time management (they wanted to spend less time in the business), by reviewing their operational structure and making the required changes.

As you can see, communicating with your potential clients about *'value'* is far more important and relevant to them. Does £2,000 a month sounds so much now for what I was offering? However, again a warning, do it from a position of authenticity and integrity.

I learnt the above from a famous consultant called Alan Weiss (he wrote a great book called *Million Dollar Consulting*), a recommended read.

Price

After I explain to clients all the value I could be offering them, I only then state my fees. I will often give three or four options with different service packages.

- **Low fee** – basic package
- **Mid fee** – standard package
- **High fee** – premium package

I also sometimes offer a 4th option if a potential client cannot afford the above fees. I call this my 'creative fee option'.

My fees are not cheap (because I offer so much value to my clients), so by offering 3 or 4 options it allows clients to purchase at a price that suits them. Note I do not discount the fee, I just provide less for a reduced fee (e.g. 1 coaching call instead of 3 calls a month).

Ending a conversation

After price, I will then revert back to talking about value and the potential for their business and their dreams. I always finish conversations from a position of possibility and value, not price.

> *"Always finish conversations from a position of possibility and value, not price."*

Story 2: Providing value in action

I had a client who was a retailer. She was working mainly on high end products and was struggling to make her business work. I was employed as her accountant

Having decided to change my business focus to business coaching/consultancy, I told her I could no longer provide pure accounting services to her as I was focusing on a more service-based value offering. We agreed to part ways, however I told her I was focused on providing her value in her business and to call me if she ever needed help.

In the months to follow, every so often she would call me or I would email her with information that I had come across relevant to her. The key thing, it was authentic and it was all about supporting her in her business. I was not trying to 'get' her as a client.

2 months later, she did became my client again, this time I secured fees which were 4 times higher then before. The value I was giving her was far in excess of the new increased fee. She was getting more value and she was happy to pay for it.

HABIT THREE

CREATE VS BEING REPORTED ON

Will you take control of your destiny and take action to create it?

"Being proactive – we can choose how we will respond to any given situation"

We can live life in two ways. We can live in a:

Reported on World
Or
Created World

What do I mean by this? Well many people live their lives reacting out of the external environment. Things happen to them and they react. They are living in a *Reported on World*. But what you should actually do is always be in creation mode and be living in a *Created World*.

Wake up each day thinking:

'What can I create today?'

(Actually along with that I also ask *'who can I serve today?'*) Then spend time doing that. Whatever that is.

Regardless of where you are, whether in your business or in life generally, you have the choice of what is next. Get creative and YOU can decide what happens in your business, right now in this moment. If you're not getting what you want then do something about it. Now.

Do it from a position of fun and excitement wherever possible. Ask other people to contribute ideas and enjoy the process. Creativity can be really fun in the way that a child does it.

Action

And… once you have been creative, you MUST take action. If there is one weakness I have seen in many businesses it is the weakness of not taking action. You have an idea, a thought but there is no follow through.

Inaction is a decision within itself.

Failure to take action is something I refuse to buy into with my clients. If anything, I refuse to work with clients who do not act, and commitment upfront is essential for the people I work with.

Importantly, I do this because it *serves* them.

Games and challenges

And to get people to create and act, I focus on games and challenges. So I often ask my clients to play games or I set them challenges as it gets them out of their heads into motion.

A simple game for example would be, go out and propose fees of £20,000 in a 3 month period. Or go out and have 10 conversations with people this week.

Up for the challenge yourself? What would you like to create? What challenge or game do you want to play? Decide and then go and do it!

> ### Story 3: Creation in action
>
> A little story. There were 8 frogs sitting on a ledge and 7 decided to jump off.
>
> How many frogs were left on the ledge?
>
> One right?
>
> No. There are still 8. No frogs had actually jumped off yet.
>
> Go ahead, stop 'deciding' and go and actually do what you want to create and do.

HABIT FOUR

FEEL THE FEAR... AND DO IT ANYWAY

Are you willing to collect more 'No's' then anyone else?

"What we fear can hide what most excites us"

Feel the fear and do it anyway, a famous saying in a famous book of the same name (look it up on Amazon if you have not heard of it). And it is so true.

What is fear? I think we have all had experiences of what it is. But did you know it is sometimes the flip side of excitement? It overlaps. What I find is when we push ourselves to seek what scares us AND excites us, that is the direction we need to head and move towards. It is where we can reach our potential.

In life we simply hold back too much and do not step into our fears enough.

So do the things you really want that scare you, ask people for things that you have never asked before, say things to people that your fearful to say, and make that bold request that is so bold you feel the fear and shiver in your body.

Lean into your edge

As my own coach says to me, *'lean into your edge',* close and even onto the edge but not so far that you fall over. For me public speaking has been one of my edges, which I am now leaning into more and more. The more I do, the edge keeps moving out. And what was initially perceived as fear, has now become excitement. I now love it (well mostly!).

And once you do lean in, through action or experience, you become confident in that thing. That is my 'secret tool' for gaining confidence of any aspect of your life – action in doing whatever you're not confident in. Do it once, twice, 50, 100 times. Once you do it enough times you will have the confidence.

What is your edge? How can you lean into it? Find it and then go and do it.

So what sort of fears come up in business and where can you face your fears and do it anyway?

- Make that phone call to someone who is much more senior to you in qualification and experience, and ask for a meeting with them (but remember get 'interested' in them first).

- Put out that first ever blog or make that first video to the whole world. And don't wait for perfection, do it anyway.

- Tell people you are the 'expert' in your field (language is powerful). Knowing 10%-20% more than who you are communicating with is usually enough.

- Speak out and present to 5 people, then 10, 25, and finally 50. When you're comfortable with that, double it to 100 and then go for an even scarier 1,000.

- State double your normal fees to the next person you want to work with. Once someone says yes to those fees, double your fees again. Once you're comfortable with that, do it again once more.

You see the pattern?

> **Story 4: Facing your fears in action**
>
> I often set my clients and myself the *'failure game'*. Go out and collect as many 'no's' and fail as many times possible. There is a time limit – often 1 week.
>
> Just this week, a client played the game and they went out and failed 5 times, things that were leaning into their edge. In failing 5 times, they also succeeded 7 times.
>
> The ultimate goal for your business is not to fail but to succeed. But failure is the path to follow in order to succeed. And remember yes lives in the land of no.
>
> Go out and fail and get a no (or two) today.

"Failure is the path to follow in order to succeed... and remember yes lives in the land of no."

HABIT FIVE

LEADERSHIP

In yourself and others

"But all of them will take their cue from you. You show loyalty, they learn loyalty, you show them it's about the work, it will be about the work. You show them some other kind of game then that's the game they'll play"

I now love learning about leadership. It is now at the cornerstone of everything I do.

But it never used to be.

You may think, well I am just starting out in business, do I really need to think about leadership? Yes. Leadership is really about leading yourself first then after that leading others. If you're starting a business or building it further, it is ALL about leadership from the moment you get out of bed each morning (what time do YOU decide to get up? That is leadership!).

Leadership defined

My own preferred definition of leadership is that it is about creating as many impactful moments, where any interaction you have with someone creates a positive impact in their lives. That could mean both small or big life changing moments. And you often may never get to know about it. What that means is anyone can choose to be a leader in whatever they do in their life. Watch the video 'lollipop moments' (Google it) to get what I really mean.

Furthermore, importantly, leadership is about creating other leaders not creating followers.

Creating the impossible and the glimpe of genius

The job of leadership is also to inspire people to dream big and 'create the impossible' - to think outside of their current thinking and give them insights into what they believe might never be possible. And once they have created this awareness, it's about supporting them on that path to get there.

And equally to see the power in people, what I call looking for the 'glimpse of genius'. Once identified it is a job for leaders to bring this awareness of peoples incredible nature to their attention, and then inspiring them to do even greater things with it.

Leading – what else?

And it does not stop there. There is more. Leadership is about:

- **Being proactive and creating something** that does not currently exist in your own or other peoples' lives (remember we live in a 'created world').

- **Inspiring and empowering others** through your conversation and actions by creating impactful moments. That could mean anything from something simple like demonstrating gratitude or kindness to something bigger like creating a life changing moment.

- **Going first**. Don't wait for others to do what you want them to do, go first and show them first by your own actions.

- **Serving rather than pleasing people**. Saying and doing things that may be uncomfortable at the time but will benefit both you and others in the longer term (think of how you do this with children).

- **Asking for what you really want**. Ask for what you want, as we are often just one step away from getting what we want – we just need to ask.

- **Not giving people answers but coaching them** to get them to answer their own questions. I answer your question, the answer belongs to me. You answer your own question, the answer then belongs to you.

Finally *'be you'*. This one is powerful. Be open and authentic about who YOU really are and what you stand for. Live by your own values, not other peoples, and importantly don't be afraid to bring your own unique personality to the world. Therein lies your power. There is only one you. You're special. You matter.

> *"Leadership is about creating other leaders not creating followers"*

Story 5: Leading in action

I have always been a bit of a follower when I worked in the corporate world for over 10 years. I would do as I was told. I followed whomever I was reporting to. Again and again. Not surprisingly, I felt I never really succeeded in my corporate career.

Then when I decided to leave the corporate world, leaving my career and flying out overseas to volunteer for 4 months, a few signs of leadership began to come through. However, even then in these months I felt I often followed.

It was only really when I decided to start my own business, I started to lead myself, more and more. And then finally leading others. It changed everything.

I would regularly ask myself how to lead by answering these questions to myself (and to others):

- Where shall I decide to take my career (and my life)?
- What are my highest values I want to follow in my career (and in my life)?
- What can I create today?
- Who can I serve today?

And what I love about all this? Now I have left my corporate career, I now spend time with people who I want to spend time with. And I serve those that I want to serve.

"Leadership is about creating as many impactful moments"

HABIT SIX

THE POWER OF LANGUAGE

Questions, questions, questions

"The question is the answer"

Is language not so powerful?

Of course it is, if used in the right way, authentically and with the right intention. Not to manipulate but to persuade and influence.

So how should you use it?

Questioning

Start any conversation with questions. Questions are so powerful. And people love to talk. Remember Gladstone from part 1? *Get 'interested'.*

And importantly, do not underestimate the power of *silence*. Let THEM speak. Even pause when you feel you want to speak. The most important point of a conversation can often arise in those powerful moments of silence. Really.

Some key questions that I love asking that are impactful to whoever you're talking to. Try it with anyone (personal or business related) and you will realise their power.

1. What do you want? What do you really want?

My first favourite question to ask a potential client. Don't just start saying what your services are. Find out first what *they* want. And then what they REALLY want.

Importantly keep searching for the *'goal behind the goal'*. Keep digging until you get to their real wants, fears, desires and dreams. For example I often ask *'once you have all the money you need, then what would that give you? What would you then actually want?'*.

2. What is important to you about [insert name of product/service you're providing]?

Another favourite question of mine. This is finding out the 'values' of what you are offering, what is important to them in their purchase. So if they are buying a car for instance, then it might be the visual aspects, the way it feels or even the power. It could be they don't really care about any of these and it is about obtaining the lowest price.

Whatever they say to the above 2 questions (and different people will say different things), you can then tailor your response to what THEY really want and what they consider is important. If for instance you called me after reading my book, I would first ask you what was *really important* about what you had read and what you really wanted help with. I would then be able to tailor my responses and provide advice according to your specific needs.

Get it?

3. What else?

This is such a key question and please don't underestimate it. Don't only believe in people's first responses to a question. So I often ask a follow up of *'what else?'*. There is often more that lies underneath the surface.

4. What if?

I love the 'what if' question (or even sometimes just starting a sentence with the word 'if'). It allows the person your asking it to, to imagine, to dream, to state what they really want their business to look like. Sometimes I ask it in the form:

'If in 3 years time your business is how you want it to be, describe to me how it will look?'

The power of imagination. Go on, get your clients to imagine.

5. Other questions

There are so many more (I have a list of over 100!) but a few others that I really like:

- What is stopping you from achieving 'x'?
- What would make this an extraordinary conversation?
- What would you love to do/what would you love to create?
- What don't you want me to know about you/What do you want me to know about you?

Story telling and impact

I love telling stories, it is so much better than hard facts. But tell stories in 'impact' terms. So don't just explain what 'you do' but explain what impact you will have on client lives and their businesses. So I often tell people about clients I work with where I consistently save them thousands of £s from key insights like increasing prices, negotiating with suppliers, connecting them to experts in different fields and saving them tax.

Always focus on impact and value, not just what you do.

Finally... don't answer their questions!

Clients will often ask me lots of questions – how to build a business, increase their sales, work less hours etc. A key piece of advice - you don't always need to answer the questions your clients ask you. Seek out the real question behind their question. What do they actually REALLY want to know?

> *"Do not underestimate the power of silence. Let them speak. Even pause when you feel you want to speak. It can be powerful."*

Story 6: SPIN selling

SPIN selling is a great book for those looking to sell high value items. There are 4 areas to selling in the SPIN cycle (a mnemonic) that you need to follow in a set order, moving from problem to solution:

1. **Situation** – ask clients a few background questions on their business (and themselves)

2. **Problem** – ask clients around the problems in their business, to uncover their needs

3. **Implications** – ask clients about the implication of the problems they are having

4. **Need-value payoff** – ask clients to describe the benefits of a solution (i.e. value)

I use it as a good framework when working with any client. Buy the book and it will offer some really good questioning techniques and language structures.

Remember language and questions are powerful.

HABIT SEVEN

SUPPORT

Do what you do best and outsource the rest

"We were young, but we had good advice... our success has really been based on partnerships from the very beginning"

– Bill Gates

What are you best at? What are you worst at?

There are just so many areas to work on in a business:

- Strategy
- Operations
- Sales and marketing
- Finance
- Human resources/employing staff
- Administration

Usually a lot of people are good in 1-2 areas. Often it is the operations side as this is why they started the business in the first place. Yet when starting out they decide, usually due to cost reasons, to do it all themselves. They can't 'afford' to hire other people. This causes problems and they spend YEARS struggling in their business.

Having self awareness is thus so key. Really understand what you are good and not so good at. What is it for you? The sales and marketing? Maybe it is the finance? Or the administration?

Outsource

Then get someone to take care of the things you're not so good at. Or at least ask for support in that area. Starting off, that can include free advice, advice from friends, family, the internet, your local accountant. Eventually hire paid specialist help in those areas which are most critical for your business. It will make a massive difference to your business.

Story 7: Outsourcing in action

I was with a client who said they knew nothing about sales and marketing. Yet they continued to work on this themselves with little success. Two years later they were still making only £10,000 a year in revenue. Finally, they decided to get some help. They did their research, interviewed 4 businesses and then hired a sales consultant. Their sales within 12 months increased by 300% to £40,000 a year.

Another company, who said they were not good at business, hired a business coach for £1,000 a month. Their largest client at the time had been £200 a month. As a direct result of coaching, they pitched £1,000 a month and won the contract. Now they had the skills, they could do it themselves again and again. And they did. Again and again.

WHAT DO YOU DO AND WHERE DO YOU GO NEXT?

What is the first thing you should do right now?

"One insight, followed by one action can change everything"

What do you do next? What did you take from this book? Nothing? Everything? Do you read this and just think, next book?

Stop. Pause. And then go back to the beginning and read this book again (or at least the areas that stood out for you).

And once you have done that, do it again. Then ask yourself the following (arguably the most powerful questions that you can ask yourself after learning something new whether from a book, a course or in a conversation):

> *'What is the one key learning I got from this?'*
> AND
> *'What is the one action I will take as a result of this learning?'*

What happens next is even more important. Go and act on it. Don't be the frogs. If you missed it, that was from chapter 3 (which you shouldn't have as you have now read the book 3 times).

And I also recommend do one new thing (however small) every day. As they say, you eat an elephant one bite at a time (sorry for the elephants out there!).

Story 8: What to do next

When people say to me they want to create a £1 million business, I ask them how much they really want it on a scale of 1 to 10.

If it is between 1-6, I ask them what they need to do to make it at least an 8. If they don't know then I ask them to come back to me when they know (or sometimes I coach them personally before I coach them on their business). I only work with people and clients who want something that is at least an 8.

So I ask all my clients to make a commitment to themselves. I get them to watch a powerful video on this called 'because I said I would' **(www.becauseisaidiwould.com).**

Are you committed to take action and do something after reading this book? If not watch this video. Then make your commitment.

In desire and motivation there is action. And in that, there must also be commitment.

"Make a commitment... because I said I would"

THE 7 STEP ACTION PLAN TO GET YOU STARTED?

The key is to start

"Inaction is a decision within itself"

If you are keen to implement the 7 habits in this book, here are 7 tasks to get you going…

Habit 1: Serve people

Think of 5 people you know and brainstorm 2 actions you can do to support each of them, things that will really help them. Then spend a week reaching out to each of them and doing one of those things.

Habit 2: Value, value value

List 10 ways you can provide value to a single client/potential client/friend of yours. In answering this, ask yourself the question 'what else?'

Reflect on the list you come up with. What price would you now put on all this value?

Habit 3: Create v Reported on World

Answer the question, 'What is impossible, which if it was actually possible, would make your life a success/create happiness for you?' List 3 things.

Next, for each of these answers ask yourself 'what would make each of these possible?'

Habit 4: Feel the Fear… and do it.

Of the items in the previous step, think of a fear that lies underneath each of them. What small step could you take to start to overcome them.

Habit 5: Leadership

Google and watch the video on leadership called 'lollipop moments'. Reflect on how the habit 1 task you did above shows signs of this type of leadership.

Of the 5 people you identified in habit 1, list 2 strengths each of these people have ('the glimpse of genius'). Tell them them these strengths when you next speak to them.

Next, get them to think outside of their current level of thinking ('create the impossible') by asking them the questions in Habit 3 above about impossible goals.

Habit 6: Questions

In your next conversation with a friend or loved one, ask the following questions:

1. What do you really want in respect of your career/relationship? What else?
2. What is important to you about all this? What else?
3. What is stopping you achieving all this? What else?

Habit 7: Support

Review Chapter 7 and list 2 areas in your business where you need most support/are not good at? What type of external support could you get in these areas?

Insight/actions from this book

Answer the following:

- 'What are the 2 key learning I got from this book?'
- 'What are the 2 key actions I will take as a result of these learning?

www.ingramcontent.com/pod-product-compliance
Lightning Source LLC
Chambersburg PA
CBHW040329220526
45473CB00009B/2620